# DEVELOPING GODLY CHARACTER FOR A HIGHER ALTITUDE

HEALTHY CHURCH BIBLE STUDY SERIES

**Volume Two**

BY

**ADEBAYO S. DAVID**

Paperbook ISBN: 978-1-952098-15-4



**Cornerstone Publishing**
A Division of Cornerstone Creativity Group LLC
Phone: +1(516) 547-4999
info@thecornerstonepublishers.com
www.thecornerstonepublishers.com

To order bulk copies of this book or to contact the author please email: greaterthingsnow@yahoo.com

# CONTENTS

# INTRODUCTION

The HEALTHY CHURCH SERIES is a series of Bible study teachings developed to encourage pastors to build a healthy church environment, based on the word of God, where believers can grow, learn and thrive spiritually, mentally, maritally and financially in life and in the kingdom of God. This is in with Paul's admonition in

1 Timothy 3:15 to teach people how to behave in the house of God, which is the church of the living God, "THE PILLAR AND GROUND OF TRUTH".

This book is designed to ensure godly characters and attitudes in believers that can make them succeed anywhere and in all aspects of life – personal Christian walk, marriage, ministry, business, academics and relationships of any kind - knowing full well the word of God and the mind of God concerning any subject that affects their lives in Christ.

Nations and people that prosper are people who have built their lives on the "truth of life" - which is Jesus Christ. He said, "You shall know the truth and the truth shall set you free. Only the truth that you know and the truth that is revealed to you can set you free!

## STUDY 1

# DEVELOPING A TEACHABLE SPIRIT

**TEXT: PROVERBS 9:9; ISAIAH 28:1-12; 2 TIMOTHY 3:1-7**

The Christian life is a glorious one, if truly lived in Christ by observing His ways, doings and teachings (Acts 1:1). No man will be like his master, except he has first learned from his master (Luke 6:40).

However, to be able to learn, one must have a teachable spirit. This is a spirit that is ready to learn, unlearn and relearn, so that the learner can be perfect like his master and thereby obtain a higher altitude in life, business and, above all, in the kingdom of God.

### UNTEACHABLE SPIRIT: A SIGN OF THE LAST DAYS (2 TIMOTHY 3:5-7; 4:3-4)

2 Timothy 4:3-4 says, "**For the time will come when they will not endure sound doctrine, but according to their own desires, because they have itching ears, they will heap up for themselves teachers; and**

**they will turn their ears away from the truth, and be turned aside to fables."**

One of the signs of the end times is that many will not like to endure sound doctrines or sound teaching. In other words, they will be unteachable. This sign will emanate from the spirit of pride, arrogance and stubbornness. Proud people will never like to receive teaching because they believe they know it all.

Anyone who is willing to rise to a higher ground must first be willing to swallow his pride so that he can receive from his master. Jesus said, come and learn of me (Matthew 11:28-30). Any believer who wants to be all that God wants him to be, who wants to attain higher grounds in life and make heaven at last, must first put away his own ways, ideas, thinking, philosophy and wisdom and then humble himself or herself to receive from the master who is Christ Jesus.

Any member, pastor, prophet, evangelist, apostle, teacher, elder or worker in the church must be constantly learning and receiving from Christ - His words, His teachings and His ways. Never lean to your own way, but rather to the way of Christ (John 14:6; Proverbs 12:15; 14:12; 16:25).

Anyone who is unwilling to unlearn and relearn is heading for the way of death.

Therefore, to attain to higher grounds, you must allow the Holy Spirit in you! The teachable spirit starts from a humble spirit! He that is humble must be teachable.

**Pride, Enemy of a Teachable Spirit** (Isaiah 5:21)

Anyone who is proud can never learn, receive instruction or be teachable.

- A proud person is a self-destructive person and he will surely fall - Jeremiah 50:32
- A proud person is an enemy of God, Christ and His Kingdom – James 4:6
- A proud person is opposed to Christ, His Kingdom and His Church – Psalm 138:6
- A proud person is a self-willed person, who follow his own ways alone – Proverbs 16:25
- A proud person is a foolish person – Proverbs 26:12
- God breaks the proud – Job 26:12
- A proud person is an abomination to God – Proverbs 16:5

Talented and gifted people often think they know it all and that makes it difficult for them to continually expand their talent.

Being teachable is not so much about competence and mental capacity as it is about altitude. It is the desire to listen, learn and apply, it is the hunger to discover and grow.

If we are going to be a successful Christian in life, business, family, marriage and our ministry, we must desire to learn, be teachable, be ready to accept God's ways and not our ways. Never assume you know it all, no matter your level in life, business, career or ministry.

## HOW TO BE TEACHABLE

1. See every opportunity to hear the word of God as an opportunity to learn and see Christ in a new way – Romans 10:17; 1 John 2:20-27

2. Be interested even if it doesn't seem interesting – Acts 26:24-28

3. Learn to listen – Luke 2:46

4. Never argue with your teachers in public. Jesus discussed the scriptures with the teachers of the law after the service, not during the service - Luke 2:42-47

## BLESSINGS AND BENEFITS OF A TEACHABLE SPIRIT

1. When we are teachable, we receive some special benefits and blessings from God. These include:

2. We become like our master – Christ Jesus – Luke 6:40

3. We are promoted in life and God's Kingdom! - Revelation 2:26
4. We are able to teach others also – 2 Timothy 2:2
5. We are able to also bring many sons and daughters into glory – Hebrews 2:9-11
6. We are able to produce after our kind – John 15:16

## PRAYER

1. Heavenly Father, give me a tender and teachable heart that is receptive to your words and the godly instructions of the authorities you have placed over me.
2. Lord, fill me with humility so that I make myself submissive to your corrections and guidance.
3. Father, remove from me pride, stubbornness and other barriers to being teachable.

# NOTES

# NOTES

STUDY 2

# KEEPING THE UNITY OF THE SPIRIT

**TEXT: EPHESIANS 4:1-13**

If we can compare a church or an organization to a vehicle, then will realize that vision (prophecy) is the fuel that makes a vehicle move. But there is another component that is just as important -it is the oil that keeps an engine running smoothly and at the right temperature.

In God's Kingdom, there is something very powerful that performs this same "engine oil" function. Paul describes this powerful substance in our text as "unity of the Spirit" and "unity of faith".

## POWER OF UNITY

Unity takes individuals and turns them into a powerful team (Deuteronomy 32:30). It binds our energies and abilities together into a massive source of power – Psalm 133:1-3.

When we are in unity as a church, group, or an organization, our power grows exponentially to ten, fifty, and hundred times what it should have been on individual basis (Acts 2:1-8, 12-32).

It is the will of God that we must endeavor to keep the unity of the Spirit. The word "endeavor" means "to try, strive to, do all you can." So, why would God say we must endeavor to keep the unity of the Spirit? It is because the devil is after our disunity. We must not be ignorant of this. When we are disunited,

- Satan wins.
- The church loses power.
- Sinners are more than saints; hell is populated more than heaven.
- Joy is stolen and sorrow is perpetuated.
- Families are broken.
- Nations divide and disintegrate.
- The church is empty and club houses are full.
- Vices increase in the land

**(Read 2 Corinthians 2:11; Isaiah 36:10-11).**

## HINDRANCES TO UNITY

### (1) Misunderstanding – Acts 7:25, Genesis 11:5-8

When intentions and purposes are not being understood, either in an individual relationship or a corporate relationship, such as the church, there is usually division.

### (2) Perceived abuses and perceived rights - 2 Corinthians 2:11; 1 Corinthians 6:7

When there are perceived rights in the church by certain individuals, there is often division and strife. When people refuse to suffer any wrong by anybody in the Church, there will be disunity. When there are perceive abuses, or someone being taken advantage of, there will be division and strife.

### (3) Not handling offenses properly – Matthew 18:15-18

When we are offended by a fellow believer, unity will be broken, unless we handle the offense correctly.

### (4) Striving - 2 Timothy 2:24

A servant of Christ must not fight. Striving always occurs when there is a fleshly grasping after power, wealth, position and influence. This breeds an argumentative spirit.

**(5) Unjust or unfair treatment - Acts 6:1**

When there is unfair treatment and judgment, it engenders disunity.

## WAYS TO PROMOTE UNITY

**(1). We must understand the purpose of the Church, our family and the assignment before us – Acts 7:25**

An understanding of what God has called us to do will keep us focused and united, even when Satan wants to bring disunity. We can see through the eyes of the Spirit that what Satan is about to cause is not in line with our assignment and we can immediately stop him.

**(2) Understanding authority - Hebrews 13:7, 17**

Authority is hard for some people to understand. God has raised authorities in homes, the workplace and in the church. We are all equal, as brothers and sisters in Christ, but in the church, God has given authority to different people. We must obey and respect them. Any authority that you cannot stand, it is better you walk away from it, in other to allow for the peace and unity of the body.

**(3) United prayer - 1 Timothy 2:1-4; Jeremiah 10:20-21**

Anyone in leadership must be ready to pray. We cannot do anything successfully without prayer.

- Jesus prayed before choosing the twelve (Luke 6:12-16).
- Jesus rose early to pray (Mark 1:35).
- Jesus stayed all night to pray (Luke 6:12).
- Jesus told His disciples to watch and pray (Matthew 26:41).
- Jesus prayed at Lazarus' tomb (John 11:38-44).
- Jesus prayed in the Garden of Gethsemane (Luke 22:39-46).

**(4) Jesus prayed on the cross (Luke 23:34, 46).**

What this tells us therefore is that the church life, the Christian life and the leadership life must be a life of prayer. Any Church that cannot pray will be disunited, and any Church that cannot get its leaders and members to pray, is on the verge of death or disintegration.

Prayer keeps us united. If we can pray together, we can keep the devil away; then we can stay together, grow together and enlarge the Kingdom together."

**(5) Handling offenses properly – Matthew 5:23-24**

Offenses cannot but come, and they have the potential to cause disaffection and disunity. However, when offenses are properly handled, it will keep the work going and our life sweet and beautiful (Philippians 1:9-10).

### (6) Doing all things in love

Ephesians 3:17; 4:2, 15-16; 5:2; 1Thessalonians 3:12; Colossians 2:2

We must ensure that whatever we do in the house of God, family or business organization, is done in love and with the general interest and profit of all in mind.

### (7) Praying specially for leaders

1 Thessalonians 5:25; 2 Thessalonians 3:1; Hebrews 13:18; Jeremiah 42:1-3

Our leaders stand in the face of attacks, oppositions, weaknesses, temptations, trials, critical decisions and afflictions. Therefore, as believers, we must continually lift them up in prayers, so they can lead us well and not do things that will jeopardize our lives and the ministry.

Ministry leadership or even leadership of any kind - be it in the home, church, community, organization or government - is not easy. We must pray for all our leaders so that they too can help to keep the unity of the spirit and of faith.

## CONCLUSION

Finally, we must understand that one of Jesus' longest prayers, recorded in John 17, has to do with the unity of believers. We must do all individually and collectively endeavor to see the fulfilment of that prayer in our lives and our church! Endeavour to keep the unity.

## PRAYER

1. Lord, pour upon my family and church the spirit of unity.
2. Help me, Lord to be an agent of unity and not disunity wherever I find myself.
3. Father, expose and expel all forces of discord in our homes and congregation.

## NOTES

# NOTES

## STUDY 3

# REBUKE AND REPROOF OF LOVE

**TEXT: LEVITICUS 19:17-18; TITUS 2:1-7,15; HEBREWS 5:1-4**

Humans are bound to make mistakes, go off-track and sometimes even go into sin. But we, as believers, are not to act as if it is none of our business. The word of God permits us to reprove our neighbors for their sin; otherwise we become partakers of their wrongdoing.

If we really love God, we will feel bound to reprove those who hate, abuse, and break His command (Ephesians 5:11). If I love the government of this country, won't I reprove and rebuke a man who abuses or breaks the law? If a child loves his parents, won't he reprove a man who abuses his parents?

If a man loves the universe and is motivated by the love of God, he knows that evil and pollution are inconsistent with the highest good of the universe. If not counteracted sin will injure and ruin our very nature. Sin tolerated is destruction in the making. Its direct tendency is to overthrow the order and destroy the happiness of the church or the universe.

Therefore, for a genuine Christian, his benevolence will lead him to reprove and oppose sin.

## RULES FOR REPROOF AND REBUKE

### 1. Love your neighbor sincerely – Matthew 5:43-48; 19:19

Love for the particular people with whom you are connected should lead you to reprove sin. "Sin is a reproach to any people" (Proverbs 14:34). Any man who commits sin also helps produce a society and an organization harmful to everything good. Such example corrupts society, destroys its peace and introduces disorder.

The word of God encourages believer to speak to their neighbors in love about their sin, to reprove them. It is not to judge them, but rather reprove them to correction, lest they are destroyed or they destroy themselves (Ezekiel 33:7-8; 2 John 1:5-6)

### 2. Throw arrows of light - Psalm 141:5; Acts 9:1-16; 2 Peter 2:1-16

We must understand as believers that one of the challenges of love is rebuke and reproof. Reproof and rebuke are made to bring a man back from the path of destruction, and back to the path of light and life.

When God confronted Saul on the road to Damascus, He confronted him with the "arrows of light" of the truth about his life, his errors and it showed him his need for repentance. It was not judgmental. Sometimes, people are doing evil and they think they are doing right (John 16:1-4).

When God correct us, it is with the intention of shining His light of truth into the darkness of our errors, sins, and unrighteousness. This is only with the intention to bring us back into His truth and life.

When we confront our neighbor or fellow believer with the mind of rebuking and reproving them, it must be with the intention of throwing arrows of light that will bring godly sorrows, repentance, and change.

### 3. Reprove with wisdom (1 Timothy 5:1-4)

Your relationship to the person who is committing sin should be properly regarded. If a child is going to reprove a parent, he should do it in a manner suited to the relationship. If a man is going to reprove an elder, it should be with all decorum of humility and love. We rebuke not to shame but to correct and restore. We shame when there is no repentant attitude (2 Thessalonians 3:14-15).

The Apostle Paul said that when rebuking an "elder" (from the Greek, "presbooteros", which means older man, Christian elder, pastor, bishop or a member of the celestial council) we must "entreat" (treat) him as a father.

Therefore, we must take into consideration the level of authority and age of those whom we are rebuking. Pastors and other leaders in church have the authority to reprove those who err and are out of the way (James 5:19-20 – that is, those who are not doing right with God and others in the church). We rebuke to keep the church healthy and not give room to the devil.

**4. Pull them from the fire of eternal destruction (Jude 1:21-23)**

We must not talk and make mockery of peoples sins; rather we go and talk to them about it. Therefore, evangelism and soul-winning is important. The ministry of reconciliation back to God is committed into our hands and not the ministry of condemnation. Some Christians often talk about people's sins behind them. This is wickedness and gossip. If you want to talk about people's sins, go and talk to them about it, and try to get them to repent and forsake them. Do not talk to others behind their back and leave them bound for hell.

Apostle Jude said in Jude 1:22-23, "**And of some have compassion, making a difference: And others save with fear, pulling them out of the fire; hating even the garment spotted by the flesh.**"

Our rebuke and reproof must make a difference in the

sinner's life. We must prayerfully pursue, rebuke and reprove in order to make a difference

Let us also take special note of the word *"pulling"*:

- To pull requires efforts
- To pull requires patience
- To pull requires consistency
- To pull requires wisdom.

So, the challenge of love, for rebuke and reproof requires effort.

To drag a man out of hell fire, we must exact effort, patience, consistency and wisdom.

The aim and end of reproof is to pull the sinners out of hell fire and this can only be done by an act of love.

**5. Whom not to reprove or rebuke** (Proverbs 9:8)

We are to reprove all men for their sin or sinful acts; but God who made the rules and the law makes an exception to the rule. This is found in our text above:

**"Do not correct a scoffer, lest he hate you"**

A man that is known to be a scoffer, a despiser, a know-it-all, an unrepentant law-breaker, a hardhearted self-willed believer, a God-hater and a despiser of religion and hater of God's will, will only provoke a quarrel without any good resulting from it when you rebuke them. Therefore, God makes such a character an exception to the rule. Such men should never be rebuked. They are swine that cherish not holy things or a righteous rebuke or reproof (Matthew 7:6).

King David talks about the righteous rebuking him (Psalms 141:5) and him not getting offended. When a man is corrected and he will not hear a righteous rebuke, such a man is a scoffer and a spiritual idolater, who has turned to the idols of his heart. Such men should be left alone (Hosea 4: 6-17)

## CONCLUSION

Conclusively, when you reprove your neighbor for sin, make him feel that it is not a personal controversy with you or a matter of judgment on your part. Don't claim any right or superiority over him, but reprove him in the name of the Lord, for the honor of God, in love, and without any sense of holier-than-thou attitude. Afterward, all rebuke is kept personal between you and him. Not a thing to be gloated over! Never say to him or her before people: "Did I not tell you?" This can be demeaning, and robbing them of their self-worth. This is not love, as it can further put them into hell fire instead of pulling them out of it! Avoid wounding your neighbor while you are on the path of reproof!

## PRAYER

1. Oh Lord, help me to love my neighbor enough to reprove and rebuke him or her when I notice any evil in or around him or her.

2. Oh Lord, give me wisdom to reprove and rebuke in love! – James 5:20

3. Oh Lord, as I am reproving and rebuking others in love, help me to keep myself pure and save myself also –Jude 1:21, 1John 5:21

## NOTES

# NOTES

## STUDY 4

# BEWARE OF WOLVES

### TEXT: ACTS 20:28-30; MATTHEW 7:15-23

Wolves and little foxes (Songs 2:15) are undeniable realities of life. They are out there to destroy the plans of God for our lives. These dangerous invaders come in different shapes into the various aspects of our lives. They come to our businesses, marriages, relationships and churches but by the grace of God, their works shall be exposed and frustrated.

### FALSE APPEARANCE OF WOLVES – MATTHEW 7:15-23

Jesus gave a clear and stern warning to watch out for wolves! This warning calls for discernment. This is because not only did He make it clear that these wolves would come and be among us, but He also said that they would not appear as wolves or foxes, but as sheep (Matthew 7:15)

## CHARACTERISTICS OF WOLVES-MATTHEW 7:16

The devil is very subtle. When he sets out to catch a believer, he never sets out as devil, or one who is dangerous; rather he transforms himself to be like an angel of light (2 Corinthians 11:14-15). This is why, for any believer who wants to overcome in these last days, Jesus clearly warns that we need watchfulness (discernment) and prayerfulness (spirituality).

Jesus specifically said we will be able to distinguish wolves from sheep by their fruits (character). Even through a wolf can wear a sheep's clothing, a wolf cannot change his character, works and appetite.

## THREE THINGS QUICKLY BETRAY A WOLF THAT IT IS NOT A SHEEP

1. Wolves do not like to lie down in green pastures. Their nature is to roam about looking for whom to devour – Psalm 23:2

2. Wolves drink from any kind of water, especially troubled waters. Sheep only drink from still waters –Psalm 23:2

3. Wolves are always "red-eyed" (bloodshot eyes) – which represents being full of anger, rage, greed, covetousness and rioting. Sheep's are "white-eyed" – showing that they are peace-loving and peace-seeking.

4. Wolves don't eat grass. The word of God is likened to green grass or green pastures (Psalm 23:2). Wolves feed on flesh and blood. They are carnivorous.

5. Wolves steal from the flock and run away. Sheep feed on what the shepherd gives them. (John 10:10).

If your life, business, ministry and church will not be destroyed, you must watch out for wolves in your life.

- There are wolves among your friends.
- There are wolves among your business partners, looking for a way to steal all your fortunes.
- There are wolves around you marriage –seeking for a way to take your spouse.
- There are wolves in the church among your eldership and membership, looking for a way to split the church. Watch out for wolves!

## FURTHER ATTRIBUTES OF WOLVES

1. They pretend to be in the know or have some sort of "inside" information – Psalm 22:16; 55:12-13.
2. They claim to be closer to God than other people, even though their behavior and speech reveal otherwise – Isaiah 29:13; Matthew 15:8; Ezek.33:31
3. They speak with bitterness, even though they claim to be speaking the truth. They claim the Holy Spirit

asks them to speak the whole truth – however, their "Holy Spirit" is questionable – 1 John 4:1

4. They claim superior supernatural wisdom and they say they belong to a special group - James 3:14-16
5. They never have your best interest at heart, their intention and motive is all about self-interest – 1 Timothy 3:2
6. They are after filthy gain! – Jude 1:11
7. They are after their own interest first before the collective interest of others – Philippians 2:20-21

## RECOGNIZING WOLVES IN THE CHURCH

Wolves in the church have identifiable characteristics through their roles. These roles include:

1. Splitting the flock
2. Stirring up rebellion
3. Accusing and antagonizing authority
4. Complaining and blackmailing without preferring solutions
5. Causing members to stumble and leading them astray

## PRAYER

1. Lord God, open my eyes of understanding to be able to discern wolves around me.
2. Father, keep my church and home from the activities of wolves and little foxes.
3. Lord, stop every negative influence in your church and let all captives of wolves be delivered, in Jesus' name.

## NOTES

## NOTES

## STUDY 5

# THE CHRISTIAN HOME

**TEXT: GENESIS 2:18; PROVERBS 5:18-19; 18:22;19:14; HEBREW 13:4; ECCLESIASTES 9:7-9**

Marriage is as fragile as the heart of a man. The state of a person's heart (the physical organ) has a positive or negative effect on the entire body. Likewise, the Christian's home can either make or mar his or her destiny.

A family, according to the Scripture, is made of the husband, the wife and the children. And that unit is the foundation stone on which every other institution in the society is built (the school, the government, the church and so on).

Therefore, the issues of marriage and family life cannot be overemphasized. Sadly, most of our Christian homes are falling below God's standard. Yet, it is expected of us to be role models for the church and the society.

### THE CONCEPT OF MARRIAGE

God is the originator of marriage. He initiated the concept and practice from the time of the creation

(Genesis 2:18-25). This means that the concept of marriage predates the fall of man. From the Scripture, we understand that:

- Marriage is both headship and helpmate – Genesis 2:18, Ephesians 5:23
- Marriage is love and submission – Ephesians 5:22-25
- Marriage requires leaving and cleaving – Matthew 19:5
- Marriage is the portrait of Christ and His Church – Ephesians 5:25
- Marriage is for partnership, pleasure, purity, protection and procreation - Heb.13:4
- Marriage is a weapon of battle against the enemies (Deuteronomy 32:30).

## CHARACTERISTICS OF MARRIAGE KEEPERS

Covenant keepers are marriage keepers because unfaithfulness kills the joy and happiness of the home. It is clear that marriage is a journey of life that experience ups and downs; nevertheless marriage keepers have certain attributes and practices that make their marriage withstand the storms of life. Let's examine these attributes and practices with the acronym, KEEPERS:

- Knowing each more and more every day.
- Experiencing God in prayers and His word.
- Encouraging each another with hope-building words.
- Praying against the enemies of your marriage.
- Excelling in mutual love, respect, consideration and faithfulness.
- Resolving issues peacefully with godly wisdom.
- Satisfying each other by seeking each other's happiness at all times.

## ROLES OF A HUSBAND

A husband is a teacher. He is like a ship that travels very far and wide – which means that he must be knowledgeable and mature in thinking and approaching issues. He is the warrior that seeks how to protect and defend his home. He must also know that his headship is not for pride but for provision. Specifically plays the following roles to keep his family peaceful and prosperous:

1. He must act as a leader (the head) - Genesis 3:16; 1 Corinthians 11:3; Ephesians 5:23; 1 Pet.2:9.

2. He must love his wife – Ephesians 5:25,28,33.

3. He must care for his wife – 1 Peter 3:7.

4. He must praise his wife often – Proverbs 31:28

5. He must be thoughtful and compassionate – Proverbs 18:12
6. He must show good example – 1 Peter 5:3
7. He must not be bitter towards his wife – Colossians 3:19

## ROLE OF A WIFE

**Colossians 3:18; Ephesians 5:22,33; 1 Peter 3:1-7; Proverbs 12:25**

1. She must look unto God always.
2. She must be very sensitive and discerning.
3. She must show great wisdom during crisis.
4. She must not be force and argumentative in trying to make her husband to understand her.
5. She must pray always for her husband and family.
6. She must be a home-keeper, creative and industrious.
7. She must be concerned about looking good personally, as well the health and wellbeing of the family.

## ROLES OF CHILDREN

1. Honor their parents – Exodus 20:12; Ephesians 6:1-

3

2. Obey their parents – Colossians 3:20
3. Be submissive to their parents – Luke 2:46-52
4. 4. Make their parents proud and happy at all times – Psalm 144:12
5. Avoid resentment – Mark 11:25

## MARRIAGE KILLERS

- Disobedience to the Scripture on individual roles in the family
- Selfishness and self-centeredness
- Infidelity and unfaithfulness
- Excessive attachment to work and ministry at the expense of the home.
- Troublesome and unforgiving spirit
- Third party influence
- Personality clash

**Steps for Keeping Your Marriage Alive**

- Praying for your spouse always.
- Faith in God for overcoming your challenges.

- Faithfulness and openness towards each other.
- Settle your differences peacefully.
- Strengthening each other's faith.
- Be a giver, helper and an intercessor.
- Obey God and serve Him in all things.

## CONCLUSION

Godly marriages give birth to great families which constitute a glorious church and a God-fearing nation. Be a rapturable Christian home. The family unit was initiated by God. Therefore, men, women and children should find stability within it and should enable the spiritual growth of all its members.

## PRAYER

1. Lord, help me to be a marriage keeper, not a marriage breaker
2. Give me wisdom to build my home according to your purpose and principles.
3. Help me and my spouse build each other up, not tear down.

# NOTES

# NOTES

## STUDY 6

# DEVELOPING A RELATIONSHIP WITH THE HOLY SPIRIT

**TEXT: JOHN 14:12; 16:5-18; ACTS 1:4-8; I CORINTHIANS 2:9-16**

After His resurrection from death, Christ appeared to His disciples severally for 40 days. But before He ascended into heaven to be with the Father, He promised the disciples a special gift which He said He would ask the Father to send to them. That gift is the Holy Spirit. Jesus Christ has not left believers alone in this world. He has sent the Holy Spirit to be with us.

One important truth we must take to heart is that the Holy Spirit is indeed God (see Acts 5:3-4 and 2 Corinthians 3:17-18 for instance). God decided to show or express Himself to us as God the Father, God the Son and God the Holy Spirit. These personalities are distinct, yet they are one. They are Three-in-one, Trinity or the Godhead.

## ENTERING INTO THE RELATIONSHIP

1. The Holy Spirit is aware of our needs at every time. The business of the Holy Spirit is to impact all believers by making them open to God. The Bible says in Ephesians 5:18, “Be filled with the Holy Spirit”. In other words, believers are enjoined to have the presence of the Holy Spirit in our lives so we can be empowered to fulfil our daily assignments and commission. He is the source of power for every committed believer who wants to please God. The Holy Spirit can come when the individual believer desires and seeks Him with all interest from the inner heart (John 7:37-39; Ephesians 5:18).

2. The Holy Spirit can be received into the individual believer’s life through baptism.

This Spirit’s baptism is the way He manifest Himself in the life of a believer with overflowing power. He comes with such power that the believer burst out in tongues – a supernatural language. (Acts 2:4; 10:45-46; 19:6; 1 Corinthians 14:5,18). The Holy Spirit is received by faith as you ask (Luke 11:9-13).

## EVIDENCE OF THE SPIRIT’S PRESENCE

- Speaking in tongues
- He testifies of our relationship (Romans 8:16)

- He assists us in living a life that is pleasing to God – Galatians 5:16
- He helps us in prayer – Romans 8:26
- He empowers us for God's service
- He imparts boldness – Acts 1:8
- He guides us – Romans 8:14
- He teaches us – John 14:26
- He glorifies the Lord in our lives – John 16:13-15
- He fills us with love for others – 1 Corinthians12:12,13
- He testifies about Jesus Christ – Acts 5:30-32

## CONCLUSION

If the Lord Jesus Christ needed to be filled with the Holy Spirit, as well as the apostles and, indeed all of the early church, then we also need to be filled with the Holy Spirit. The Holy Spirit is God's gift to every believer. When a person believes in Jesus Christ and receives salvation, the Holy Spirit comes to live in him, imparting spiritual life and power (Luke 4:1,14; Acts 2:2-4; 9:17).

## PRAYER

1. Lord, fill me with your Holy Spirit and power.
2. Father remove every hindrance to the move of the Holy Spirit upon my life.
3. Lord, empower me to do uncommon exploits through the help of your Spirit.

## NOTES

## NOTES

## STUDY 7

# HOLINESS MADE SIMPLE

**TEXT: EXODUS 3:5 LEVITICUS 20:26; ISAIAH 6:3; JOHN 14:15-17; 1 PETER 1:16; REVELATION 4:8**

God is holy. Indeed, He has made Himself known to mankind as the Holy Spirit. So what is holiness? Holiness means perfection, purity, blamelessness, and spiritual excellence. God enjoins believers to maintain a life of holiness which is a reflection of our call and new life in Christ. This we cannot achieve on own but through the help of the Holy Spirit. God's standard of holiness can be achieved by believers coming into a relationship with God through Christ's redemption work accomplished on the Cross (Romans 12:2; 1 Peter 1:13-16).

### GOD'S DEMAND FOR HOLINESS

We belong to a holy household as members of God's family. Our Father – Yahweh, the head of the family - is holy. Therefore it behooves us children of this heavenly household to live holily. By this, people will see us as separated royal priesthood unto God (Ephesians 1:4; 1 Peter 1:14-16; 2:9)

## COMMITMENT TO HOLINESS

The Father took it upon Himself for us to be holy through the sacrificial offering of Christ on our behalf. It is therefore our responsibility to sacrifice everything in order to live as He does. We must obey His commandments and commit ourselves to walk in the newness of life, created in the likeness of God in true righteousness and holiness (Deuteronomy 26:16-19, Ephesians 4:24; 1 John 2:6).

## STEPS TO HOLINESS

1. Sanctification and consecration – 1 Peter 1:2; 1 Thessalonians 5:23
2. Be in Christ - 1 Corinthians 1:2
3. Receive the cleansing of the blood of Jesus – Hebrews 13:12
4. Have faith in Christ – Acts 26:18
5. Let Christ empower you – 1 Thessalonians 3:13
6. Get the truth of God's word – John 17:17
7. Embrace righteousness – Romans 6:19,22

8. Receive the fire of the Holy Spirit – Matthew 3:11-12
9. Be disciplined – Hebrews 12:10
10. Strive to be holy - Hebrews 12:14

## SUSTAINING HOLINESS

1. Walk in righteousness – Romans 8:1-4
2. Be spiritually minded – Romans 8:5-9
3. Renew your mind and consecration – Romans 12:1, 2
4. Be spiritually conscious – Romans 13:11-14
5. Keep reading and studying God's word – John 8:47 a; Rom.10:17
6. Be guided by the spirit – Galatians 5:16-18
7. Resist pressure of the flesh – Galatians 5:19-21
8. Love not the world – 1John 2:15-17
9. Determine to live a holy life – Psalm 51:10-12; 1 Peter 1:2
10. Preach the Word – Acts 1:8; 4:31; Mark16:15
11. Teach the word – Matthew 28:19-20.

## PRAYER

1. Lord, cleanse and purify me from all filthiness with the blood of Jesus.
2. I consecrate myself to you today, Lord, make me a vessel of honor unto yourself.
3. Lord, fill me with grace to abstain from all appearance of evil.

## NOTES

# NOTES

## STUDY 8

# THE ROYAL LAW

### TEXT: JAMES 2:1-13

Most people have heard the expression, "Love your neighbor as yourself" but not many realize that this is more than a suggestion or a quotable quote. While Jesus was speaking to the teachers of the law, the scribes and the lawyers in Matthew 22:35-40, one asked Him what the greatest commandment is (verse 35-36). Jesus said to him, "You shall love the Lord your God with all your heart, with all your soul, and with all your mind.' This is the first and great commandment. And the second is like it: 'You shall love your neighbor as yourself.' On these two commandments hang all the Law and the Prophets."

Jesus clearly stated that the greatest commandment is to love God with all we have. But He also added that the second greatest is to love our neighbor as ourselves. This is what Apostle James called "The Royal Law" in James 2:8.

## DEFINING THE ROYAL LAW

### James 2:1-4, 8

Loving our neighbors as ourselves did not originate in the New Testament. God Himself gave the commandment to His people long before then New Testament. Leviticus 19:13-18 contains God's precepts on thoughtful and kind dealings with people around us and the people we come in contact with (referred to as our neighbors).

To love your neighbor clearly means that there are certain actions you must demonstrate towards other people and similarly there are things you must never do to them (Leviticus 19:13-18; 1 Thessalonians 4:1-12; James 2:1-4).

The Royal Law is the Law of Love. When you Love God, you must love your neighbors. In fact, Jesus took this further by saying you must also love your enemies! (Matthew 5:44-48). Hard? Yea and nay! (1 John 5:3). This commandment is hard for those who are not born-again, it is hard for the carnal minded, the unsanctified, the unregenerate, the unconverted, the unrepentant and the unbroken! But to the regenerated and spiritual minded, it is possible by the Spirit.

The Royal Law in Action – 1 John 4:7-20; Leviticus 19:13-18; 1 Thessalonians 4:1-2; Matthew 5:47-48

According to the scriptures above, when you walk in the Royal Law it will be demonstrated in your actions. This means that:

1. You will never defraud (cheat) others – Leviticus 19:3
2. You will never rob others of their wages (salary and dues) – Leviticus 19:13.
3. You will not put a stumbling-block or anything that offend – Leviticus 19:14
4. Never mock those with disabilities (physical or spiritual)
5. You must not be partial in judgment - Leviticus 19:15, James 2:1-4.
6. Never bear tales about your neighbor or brethren - Leviticus 19:17.
7. Never hate your neighbor - Leviticus 19:17, 1 John 4:20
8. Rebuke your neighbor when he or she is wrong – Leviticus 19:17.
9. Never revenge against your neighbor – Leviticus 19:18
10. Never bear grudge against your neighbor – Leviticus 19:18

11. Love your enemies – Matthew 5:44

12. Bless those who persecute you – (Romans 12:14)

13. Pray for your neighbor – (Luke 6:28).

These are just few of the requirements of the Law of Love that the Lord that the Lord has given us as the Royal Law.

**The Royal Law Operation in a Local Church – James 2:1-13**

The church must have love and demonstrate the love of Christ without respect of persons. There should be no differentiation in love towards people in the congregation, towards the rich or the poor. Love must be equal (James 2:2-3). God warns about missing the mark because we tend to honor people in our congregation based on their appearance, wealth and connections. It is unscriptural or ungodly for us to treat or relate to people based on their wealth. It is the same God, both for the poor and the rich; and God wants everyone saved! (Luke 14:12-34).

The Royal Law sees God's love, God's grace and God's purpose. When we see with the eyes of God we know that:

- God has chosen the poor.
- The poor can also be rich in faith more than the financially rich.

- The poor are also heirs of the Kingdom.
- The poor can also become financially rich.
- The poor will not leave when the chips are down
- The poor can increase the work and cause the Kingdom to spread quickly
- We must not despise the poor

When we consider the Royal Law in the light of James 2:5-7 we will know that we must not spend our time trying to win only the rich, because the rich tend not to want to accept Christ quickly (Matthew 19:22-23). Secondly, many rich people tend to despise and blaspheme the name of God (James 2:7). Thirdly, the rich mostly set their heart and mind on their wealth rather than on God (Psalm 62:10). Fourthly, it is difficult for the rich to enter God's Kingdom because of obsession with their riches (Matthew 19:24); Fifthly, and thankfully, it is possible for the rich to make it to God's kingdom (Matthew 19:25-26). This means that to be rich is not a sin or a crime. There are rich people in God's kingdom today and in heaven, and there are many poor people also in hell.

- Abraham was very rich
- Isaac was very rich
- Jacob was very rich
- Joseph was very rich

- Daniel was rich
- Joseph of Arimathea was rich
- John D. Rockeffeller was rich and born again.

## CONCLUSION

Therefore, according to the Royal Law, we must treat both the poor and the rich equally (James 2:8-10). God wants the church to practice unbiased and unsegregated love for one another so that His house will be full, joyous, prosperous and progressing.

## PRAYER

1. Thank you, Lord, because you love all men equally and you want all to be saved.
2. Lord, give me the grace and wisdom to treat all men the way you want me to do.
3. Fill your church with a heart of love towards the rich and the poor, the saved and the unsaved.

# NOTES

# NOTES

## STUDY 9

# BIBLICAL REASONS WHY YOU MUST TITHE AND GIVE

### TEXT: MALACHI 3:7-18; 2 CHRONICLES 31:1-5, 11-21

It can indeed be surprising and disturbing when we as believers think we can create our own ways and shortcuts in getting into God's river of abundance and financial blessings. Let it be known that the ways of God are true and His commandments are sure. Psalm 111:7-8 says, "The works of His hands are verity and justice; All His precepts are sure. They stand fast forever and ever, And are done in truth and uprightness."

Therefore, to think that we can design our ways, apart from His own stipulated ways, will not be to our own benefit. God has designed specific ways and routes by which believers can inherit Abraham's blessings and these ways are spelt out in tithing and giving (Hebrews 7:1-10).

Abraham tithed, gave and was blessed! The Bible advises us to look unto Abraham our father and do what he did so that we can be blessed (Isaiah 51:2). Though we all sing “Abraham’s blessings are mine”, not all are doing Abraham deeds so that the blessings will be manifest.

## 10 REASONS WHY YOU MUST GIVE

1. Giving is reflects God’s nature.
    - The difference between God and Satan is that God is a giver, Satan is a taker.
    - God gives joy, peace, love, hope and life but Satan takes all of these.
2. Giving shows that you truly love –John 3:16
3. Giving impresses God (Proverbs 3:9-10). When you give an offering, it is an act of publicly honoring God (Luke 7:1-6)
4. God promises to respond back and quickly to givers (Luke 6:38).
5. Giving is an eternal proof of your real faith! (Malachi 3:10-11).
6. When you give, it is a public expression that God is important to you. When you do, you activate the exchange principle.
  - You give your sins to him, He gives forgiveness to you (1 John 1:8-9)
  - You give your confused mind, He gives you peace

of mind (John 14:27).

- You give your unclean heart, He gives you a new heart (Ezekiel 36:26).
- You release what you have, He releases what He has for you (Luke 6:38). V38

7. Your giving is your love in action (Matthew 7:11)
8. Everyone has something to give (1 Peter 4:10).
9. Do not let rejection of your gift by the unthankful to stop you from continuing to give. Sometimes, people reject your gift when they can't discern your purpose and sincerity (John 1:11).
10. God treasures the giver (Deuteronomy 26:10-11; James 1:17-18).

## 10 REASONS WHY YOU MUST TITHE IN YOUR LOCAL CHURCH

1. It is a tried and proven practice by godly people throughout all ages - Genesis 14:17-20; 28:16-22; Leviticus 27:30; Proverbs 3:9-10; Malachi 3:7-15; Matthew 23:23

   Sir John Templeton, chairman of Templeton Funds that manages over $15,000,000,000 ($15 billion) annually in investments said, "I have observed 100,000 families over my years of investment counseling. I always saw greater prosperity and happiness among those families who tithed than among those who didn't – Plus magazine Vol.43 #7 Pg.31

2. It will help you reference God more in your life – Deuteronomy 14:23.

3. It will bring God's wisdom and other blessings to your finances and will help you tame the power of materialism in your life – Matthew 6:19-21, 24-34; Luke 12:16-21; 1 Timothy 6:6-10, 17-19; Ecclesiastes 5:10.

4. It will serve as a reminder to you that God is the owner of everything in your life – 1 Chronicles 29:11-18; Psalm 24:12; Psalm 50:10-12; Haggai 2:8.

5. It will allow you to experience God's care and provisions in special ways –Proverbs 3:9-10; Haggai 1:4-11; Matthew 12:41-44

6. It will encourage your spiritual growth and trust in God – Deuteronomy14:23; 2 Corinthians 8:5

7. It will ensure your treasure in heaven – 1 Timothy 6:18-19; Matthew 6:19-21; Hebrews 6:10; 1 Samuel 30:22.

8. It will strengthen the ministry, outreach, and stability of the local church – Acts 2:42-47; 2 Corinthians 9:12-13

9. It will help provide the means to sustain the pastors

and missionaries in full time Christian service – 1 Corinthians 9:9-11; 1 Timothy 5:17-18, Philippians 4:15-19; Galatians 6:6

10. It will also help in accomplishing some soul-saving projects – Luke14:20-24; 2 Kings 12:2-16.

**Your tithe and giving is your gateway to blessings!**

## PRAYER

1. Father in heaven, fill me with grace to be a cheerful giver.
2. Lord God, take away the spirit of greed and love of money from me.
3. Lord, make my life a testimony to the wonders of cheerful giving.

# NOTES

# NOTES

## Study 10

# TAMING AND HEALING THE TONGUE

### TEXT: PROVERBS 18:21; JAMES 3:1-18

The tongue is very vital to our lives as humans. As a physical organ, it gives us the ability to taste and speak, while in the spiritual sense, the tongue controls our destinies, regardless of our statues as Christians or unbelievers.

Proverb 18:21 says death and life are in the power of the tongue. This mean that the power of curse, cancer, paralysis, failure, sickness, long-life, health and wealth are all embedded in the tongue. The tongue controls death and life. (Proverbs 13:3; 21:23).

The outcome of your life is dependent on the outflow from your month. Psalm 34:12-13 says, "Who is the man who desires life, and loves many days, that he may see good? Keep your tongue from evil, and your lips from speaking deceit."

**Controlling Your Heart and Tongue - Proverbs 12:14, 3:2, 13:3, 15:23, 18:7, 20, 21:23, Ecclesiastes 10:13.**

The heart and the tongue are cousins or twin brothers. Whatever you allow, tolerate, meditate and allow to dominate you heart, your mouth will speak. (Matthew 12:34; Luke 6:45, Jeremiah 9: 8). Whatever you say, you will have (Mark 11:23, Matthew 12:37; Proverbs 13:3; Numbers 14:28).

We must be careful not to speak any negative word, death-words, killing words and destroying words to others or to ourselves. Whatever we say, God will do. Words are seeds; you might not see their immediate result now, but sooner or later they will germinate and produce fruits.

Mind your language, and don't speak any idle, foolish or hurtful words. It is only a fool that mocks at sin (Proverbs 14:9).

**Diseases of the Tongue - James 3:1-12**

Many believers are spiritually sick because their tongues are spiritually diseased. The things that come from their mouths are nothing but poisons, death, disaster, confusion and sorrow. Their tongues are caustic and pigmented with signs of death and diseases. These diseases must be identified and healed.

**1. Excessive talking - Proverbs 10:19; Ecclesiastes 5:1-2**

This is a disease of the tongue, even though some people take it or think it as normal. When you talk too much, you sin and say nonsense. It is a sign that your tongue is very poisonous. Heaven and people can't keep secrets with you; you will betray them! (Mercy for your soul)!

- When you talk too much, it is a sign that you are a fool. Ecclesiastes 5:3
- It is only a fool that speaks all that is inside him. – Proverbs 29:11
- People who are always talking are restless people. Excessive talking is a sign of someone whose mind is not at rest - Isaiah 26:3

**(2) Idle and careless words - Matthew 12:36**

When you say things you don't mean, it is a sign that your tongue is diseased. When you join in useless discussions and words that do not edify, it means your tongue is sick and you need healing.

**(3) Gossip - Leviticus 19:16, Proverbs 18:8**

Anyone who goes about spreading slander - that is, idle, untrue, exaggerated and malicious talk – is a gossip. The word rendered "devil" in Greek means "a slanderer." So, if you gossip and tell tales, you are actually doing the devil's work for him. You need deliverance and healing.

- A gossip must be stop and not received – Proverbs 20:19, 15:1-3
- A believer must not slander
- A believer must not say evil
- A believer must not take up a reproach against his neighbor - Psalm 18:1-3
- Gossip sometimes sounds interesting but we must avoid it - Proverbs 26:20

**(4) Lying - Proverbs 6:16-19; Proverbs 12:22**

We must avoid lies - all kinds: white, green, red, black or "evangelistical"! What is evangelistical lies? 100 people came for the service, but the reports says a thousand came for the service. This is exaggeration, and exaggeration is nothing but a lie. Lying is the language of the devil (John 8:44)

**(5) Flattering tongues - Psalm 12:1-3**

There are people who flatter others. They say things that are not true, which they don't mean. Such people are diseased in their tongues and need healing (Proverbs 29:5, 26:28).

**(6) Hastiness of speech - Proverbs 29:20**

Anyone who is hasty in word, his condition is worse than a fool (Numbers 20:7-12). Hasty speech can cost us eternity and our promised blessings (Psalm 106:32-33).

A provoked spirit causes us to speak unadvisedly with our lips, and these causes us more privileges and blessings. Think of Moses and beware..

**(7) Healing the Tongue - Matthew 12:33 -35**

The root of every problem affecting the tongue is the heart. If the heart can be healed, the tongue will produce good fruits. The heart is the tree and the words are the fruit. If the heart is good, the words will be good. It the heart is evil, the words will be evil (Proverbs 4:23).

## STEPS TO HEALING THE TONGUE

1. Call your tongue problem the right name – no excuse.
2. Confess your sins.
3. Refuse to continue in the act!

You must accept the fact that you cannot tame or control your own tongue by yourself; but through the help of the Holy Spirit, you can do all things (Philippians 4:13).

**PRAYER**

1. Father touch my tongue with the coal of your fire and consume every iniquity.
2. Oh Lord, touch my heart with your fire in Jesus' name
3. Father, sanctified my spirit, soul and body
4. Lord, give me a new tongue and a new speech

# NOTES

## NOTES

**Study 11**

# SPEAKING KINGDOM LANGUAGE AND LIVING BY FAITH

**TEXT: JOSHUA 1:8; 2 CORINTHIANS 4:13; HABAKKUK 2:4; ROMANS 10:17**

The Bible says the just shall live by faith, and the believer shall have whatsoever he or she says (Habakkuk 2:4; Mark 11:23). We speak Kingdom language if we are going to prosper and flourish as Christians. The Kingdom language is the language of faith, not just hope. Hope is good, it makes not ashamed, but if we must see hope translate into reality, we must speak by faith what we hope to see (2 Corinthians 4:13).

The just live by faith and not by the gifts of the spirit. The gifts are a blessing to us, but they are to most especially convince unbelievers and bring them to the saving knowledge of Christ. The Bible does not say without the gifts of the Spirit, it is impossible to please God. It says without faith it is impossible to please God (Hebrews 11:6). So we please God by faith and we live by faith.

Therefore, faith and faith words form the Kingdom language. We are supposed to talk, walk, and live day by day by faith.

## DEVELOPING KINGDOM LANGUAGE

**Joshua 1:8, Colossians 3:16**

Just like a child growing up and learning new words through what he hears, the believer must also learn words of the Kingdom in order to speak Kingdom language. The word of God is the language of the Kingdom. Hearing it, meditating upon it, studying and speaking it, gives our spiritual vocabulary faith, power and dominion.

That is why it says in Joshua 1:8, "This book of the law shall not depart…" We must meditate on the word. To meditate is to consume the word, digest the word, regurgitate the word, speak the word to yourself and speak it to your situation.

## GOD'S WORD BUILDS FAITH SHIELD AND PROSPERITY

**Joshua 1:8, Ephesians 6:16, Romans 10:17**

The word of God creates a shield of faith around us, which is able to quench the fiery darts of the wicked. The arrows of the wicked can only be stopped by the shield of faith. Faith comes by the word of God

(Romans 10:17).

When we meditate on God's word, dwell on it, speak it and quote it, it builds a shield of faith around us, and through that, we make our way (not God) prosperous.

**Words are spirit and life (John 6:63)**

Words are spiritual forces. Words are spirit. Words created everything you can see, feel, taste, touch or hear around you (Genesis 1:1-26). God created man in His image. Therefore, man has the same capabilities of speaking spirit words that can create what he wants (Mark 11:23).

**Therefore:**

- Speak abundance before the need arises (2 Corinthians 4:13). Learn to meditate the word of God to set your system in motion before a need arises.
- Declare the word of God concerning your situation (Philippians 4:19).
- Declare your healing from sicknesses (1 Peter 2:24).
- Speak all that you desire to see in your life (Romans 10:8).
- Speak for a change in your situation (2 Corinthians 4:18).
- Avoid the snare of negativity with your mouth
- (Proverbs 18:21; Mark 11:23)

**Living by Faith (2 Corinthians 5:7)**

We must walk by the word of God and not by what our physical senses say to us or show us. Faith is the opposite of fear. Negative situations create fear, but faith gives a sound mind and that which we desire to see. (2 Timothy 1:7).

Move out fear, move into faith, which comes by hearing and studying the word (Romans 10:17). Never stop hearing the word. It shapes your thought, your belief and how you live.

If we must be successful in our Christian walk with God, and also see good all our days, we must keep speaking Kingdom language of blessings and not cursing in all situations. We must live by faith in order to get into the realms of God's glory and prosperity.

**PRAYER**

1. Oh Lord, touch my lips and let me speak the language of heaven and of Christ.

2. I believe, oh Lord, in what your word says to me.

3. I am a faith person, I live by your word and I declare your word into my life.

# NOTES

# NOTES

## Study 12

# PRAISE – THE KEY TO POWER

**TEXT: PSALM 50:23; 2 CHRONICLES 7:1-6; 8:12 -14; 20:19 -22**

Praise is the third element in the sequence of receiving from heaven. The act of asking and receiving must follow a divine pattern of asking (prayer), confession (faith) and praise, encouraging our confession or faith to become a reality.

Therefore, it is more proper to use our tongue for praise (Psalm 107:31), rather than for complaining, murmuring, gossiping and backbiting.

### SEVEN MANIFOLD POWER OF PRAISE

**1. Praise works wonders - 2 Chronicles 20-21**

When Jehoshaphat and his people praised the Lord, the Lord fought on behalf of his people and praise produced victory.

**2. Praise is the secret lubricator of faith – Isaiah 53:5**

When you believe the word of God concerning your situation, you will praise Him until the manifestation comes.

**3. Praise precedes the baptism of The spirit – Luke 24: 53**

The 120 in the upper room were praising and blessing God, before the Spirit's outpouring came.

**4. Praise brings God's presence – Psalm 22:3**

Praise brings God's presence. It drives the clouds of depression away, and lifts our spirits - especially if the praises and worship come from a truly anointed and grateful heart.

**5. Praise prospers us – Luke 3: 24. 53**

Praise keeps us humble before God. And in humility there is lifting.

**6. Praise is personal – Exodus 16:14-21**

The Scripture says, "Praise the Lord". Everyone must know how to praise God. in praising, the blessings came down.

**7. Praise puts us in time with heaven – Revelation 5:8-11**

When we praise, heaven responds. The 24 elders bow, a divine aroma is released that pervades the throne of heaven.

Praise produces a blessed refreshing from the Lord to you. You may be tired physically, but Jesus is the Resting place to those who love and praise Him. His rest is very rich and uplifting and it quickly renews both mind and body (Matthew 11:28)

## 11 FACTS ABOUT PRAISE

1) Praise unlocks heaven's portals

2) Praise causes doubt to cease

3) Praise brings precious blessings

4) Praise leaves the sweetest peace

5) Praise breaks all bonds asunder

6) Praise sets the captures free

7) Praise lightens every burden

8) Praise is a master key like prayer

9) Praise changes circumstances

10) Praise establishes the heart

11) Praise is a holy calling

## HOW DO WE PRAISE?

**Psalm 66:8; 34:1, Hebrews 13:5**

To praise the Lord requires will power and boldness. The natural flesh will not like to praise God, but as you reach forth through your spirit and arms stretch out to Him, the fills you with His presence.

**Five Reasons for lifting the hands in Praise**

1. Lifting the hands is a spiritual way of expressing thanks to God (Psalm 63:3-4),
2. lifting the hands is an appropriate way to worship God in the sanctuary (Psalm 134:2)
3. It is God's will that we worship in this way (1 Timothy 2:8).
4. It is a symbolic way of expressing ascending worship (Psalm 141: 2)
5. It is a way of expressing spiritual thirsting (Psalm 146:6)

Conclusively, if you want to see God always, never stop praising Him.

## PRAYER

Lord, endure me with the spirit and garment of praise.

# NOTES

# NOTES

## Study 13

# THE FRUIT-BEARING CHRISTIAN

### TEXT: LUKE 13:9; JOHN 15:8, GENESIS 1:24-25

The word of God is clear about the mind of God for His Children. His plan and purpose for us is to bear fruit, Increase and multiply. Whatever does not reproduces itself is close to extermination. So also is the believer in Christ. Once you are born-again, you must produce; you must bring forth fruit in the Kingdom.

### THE BELIEVER'S CALLING

The believer is likened to the branch of a tree, which produces fruit at its right season. But the branch cannot produce if it is cut off from the main tree (John 15:4). A Christian who does not continue or remain in Christ who is the Vine cannot produce or bear fruit and any branch that consistently refuses to bear fruit will be cut off and ultimately burned (Hebrews 6:7-8).

Therefore, it is the will of God that we should produce fruit. We must bear fruit in the Kingdom. We must bring forth fruit after our kind. That is when God is pleased with us (John 15:16).

There is an ability in every believer to produce and bear fruit because the seed of fruitfulness is in you. You must tap into it, release it and bear fruit. Other people must come into the Kingdom through you (1 Corinthians 4:15). Your Christian activities, your seriousness about Kingdom matters and duties will bring other souls who are not in this flock into the flock. If we are not giving birth to spiritual children, there is a serious problem.

## 10 REASONS WHY YOU MUST BEAR FRUIT

### 1. It is a proof of your being born-again – Matthew 7:20

Born-again Christians are differentiated from a counterfeit Christians through the fruits they produce. When you are bringing forth other believers and Christians like yourself, it is a sign that you are fruitful. Real Christianity takes place outside the Church on Sunday. There are many goats that must be converted into sheep; and it is expected that you bring them in, if you are truly a sheep yourself.

### 2. It shows that you are spiritually healthy - 2 Peter 1:5-8

When a woman cannot give birth, it is a sign that something is wrong somewhere. A believer who is not producing spiritual children, bringing forth other believers, is either spiritually sick, barren or malnourished.

When you grow properly spiritually, you will neither be barren nor unfruitful (2 Peter 1:8).

**3. It shows that the word of God in you is not choked or constrained - Mark 4:19**

The word of God being choked in you means that it is blocked or obstructed. When the things of this world occupy your life, you will naturally not be able to bear much fruit for God's Kingdom. But when the word has freedom and passage way in you, you definitely must bear fruit because the word will push you into conception and delivery of spiritual babies.

**4. It shows that you have overcome the forces contending against the church - 1 Corinthians 15:58**

A lot of things contend against the church - conflicts, demonic activities, prejudice and faithlessness. A believer who has overcome these will be much more fruitful than the one who still indulges in petty quarrelling, gossip, malice and all kinds of spiritual distractions.

**5. It shows that you are an active Christian**

It is not possible for a woman to want to have children, and not indulge in the activity that produces children. So, if you are going to be fruitful and bear children you must be ready to get involve in the activities that will make you fruitful such as: regular Bible study, witnessing, teaching, helping, preaching, counseling and other spiritual activities that yield result. Don't be a dormant Christian.

**6. It shows that you are mature - 2 Corinthians 13:11**

You must bear fruit to show that you are not a baby or a child. Children don't give birth, they don't have the developed womb to carry children. A Christian without a convert is immature. When you are born again you must aim to grow and have your own spiritual children.

An immature Christian runs from church to church. When you do this, it shows that you are shallow, childish and tossed to and fro.

**7. It shows that you are still abiding -John 15:4-5**

You cannot bear fruit except you abide in Christ. Abiding Christians are those who remain long enough with the Lord to be able to produce. God wants you to have a restful spirit. Be stable in the church, be permanent. Abide. Make a commitment to remain in the church. Psalm 92:13-14

**8. It brings unlimited joy -Psalm 127:3-5, John 16:21**

When you give birth as a parent, your heart if filled with joy. When you are a fruit-bearing Christian, you will have joy and heaven also will have joy over you.

### 9. It keeps you from eternal shame - Revelation 14:13

When you die in the Lord, you rest from your labors, and your works will follows you. When you die, you cannot take anything with you. The only thing that will follow you is your works.

So, when you die in the Lord and you also have fruit, you will have joy on the last day. You will not be ashamed!

### 10. It helps to preserve and multiply your own kind in the church - Genesis 7:3

Believers who bear fruits, keep seed alive. Many churches that were once fruitful and filled with people are now empty and dead without people. If we are not going to experience that, we must begin to bear fruit after our kind. Bring your kind of people to church.

- Doctors must win doctors
- Students must win students
- Nurses must win nurses
- Businessmen must win businessmen
- Lawyer must win lawyers
- Transporters must win transporters
- Farmers must win farmers

- Professionals must win professionals
- Teachers must win teachers

In conclusion, fruit-bearing must be the cry of our heart. Rachael cried to Jacob, "Give me children or I die" (Genesis 30:1).

We must cry to God to give us individually spiritual children, to present to Christ in His Kingdom.

## PRAYER

1. Oh Lord, give me grace to be fruitful.
2. Lord, revive my spiritual womb, and empower my seed to produce.
3. Oh Lord, remove every barrier to my fruitfulness.

# NOTES

## NOTES

## Study 14

# THE SIN OF BACKSLIDING

**TEXT: HOSEA 4:16; PROVERBS 14:2-14**

The sin of backsliding is a subtle sin of gradual turning away from following God. It does not happen instantly, suddenly or immediately; it slowly creeps on a believer unawares and it gradually leads him away from following God into following his own ways and worshipping his own ideas.

King Solomon says in Proverbs 14:14 that one of the marks of a backslider is that he is full of his own ways; the ways of God are no longer his ways. He does his own things as he wants, not as God wants. The ultimate danger is that a backslider will eat the fruit of his own devices which is destruction (Proverbs 1:31; 12:15).

### PORTRAIT OF THE BACKSLIDER

1. A backslider is the man who has exchange the fountain of life, living water for a broken cistern - Jeremiah 2:13.
2. A backslider is the one who has changed from a noble vine to a wild one - Jeremiah 2:21; Isaiah 5:1-7.

3. A backslider is like a wild camel; it is useless for carrying burdens - Jeremiah 2:23.
4. A backslider is like a wild ass - Jeremiah 2:24.
5. A backslider is like a lady who forget her ornaments – Jeremiah 2:32
6. A backslider is like a bride who forgets her wedding gown and appears in her night gown! - Jeremiah 2:32. How shameful can this be, as no woman forgets her wedding gown. To stay away from Christ is to forget your spiritual wedding gown.
7. A backslider is like a married man playing with a harlot! – Jeremiah 3:1
8. A backslider is like a dog eating his own vomit – Proverbs 26:11

## CAUSES OF BACKSLIDING

Not all believers fall into the sin of backsliding. Those who fall into it have certain characteristics and tendencies, which include:

1. They are shallow Christians who have no root in spiritual things. – Luke 8:13.
2. They are spiritual empty clouds without rain – I Corinthians13:1; Jude 1:12.

3. They are full of lust for the world – 2 Timothy 4:10; 1 John 2:15-17; James 4:4.

4. They are full of bitterness – Hebrews 12:15

5. They love sinful company - Proverbs 1:10

6. They don't like the truth of the word of God; it pinches them - Psalm 56:5

7. They are rebels. They rebel against God's word, God's authority and leadership - 1 Samuel 15:23

8. They are spiritually foolish, ignorant and without the knowledge of God –

9. Psalm 107:17; Proverbs 13:20.

10. They love to toy and play with sin – Proverbs 14:19

**SIGNS OF A BACKSLIDING CHRISTIAN**

1. He does not enjoy the company of believers and the righteous anymore. Church is no longer interesting to him. Activities of the world have become more exciting than the things of God. Godless people are his "fellowship" members (1 Corinthians 15:33; Psalm 1:1-3).

2. He is always remembering his past sinful life. He constantly reflects on the pleasures of his sinful life. Whereas the word of God says; we must not look back.- Philippians 3:13; Genesis 19:17.

3. He is spiritually overconfident. He believes he can never fall, having forgotten that he stands by grace.

4. He is stubborn and will only do his own thing – Proverbs 14:14; Hosea 11:7.

5. He is a forgetful Christian. He has no memory for the things of God and for the word of God. Deuteronomy 8:14; Hebrews 2:1-3

6. He neglects spiritual disciplines, such as fasting, to charge up his spiritual body and keep his flesh under – Isaiah 58:3

   Fasting keeps the believer from backsliding. It is a spiritual means of checking yourself and subduing the flesh. It keeps you on track with God and prevents spiritual coldness. It helps you stay humble and certain life's problems are solved by waiting on God in fasting and prayer (Matthew 17:21).

7. He gets angry at spiritual correction – Proverbs 9:8; Ecclesiastes 4:13

8. He allows the things of this world to get the best part of him and the word of God in him is choked through cares, worries and anxiety.- Mark 4:19

9. A backslider has a damaged conscience – Romans 2:15

10. A backslider does not enjoy prayer meetings or prayer fellowship anymore

11. He is irregular at church, always giving one excuse or the other.- Hebrews 10:25 (12) He is spiritually cold – Matthew 24:12

12. He asks foolish questions – 2 Timothy 2:23

13. He treat holy and spiritual things lightly – Matthew 7:6

14. He lacks spiritual ambition. He does not desire to grow spiritually or be used by God.- Philippians 3:13-14; Hebrews 5:12

15. He murmurs, complains and gossips about God's people – Philippians 2:14

16. He loves the company of wrongdoers – Isaiah 5:20, Malachi 2:17

17. They judge and condemn other believers – Jude 1:12-17

We need to guard our hearts diligently as believers and beware because the sin of backsliding can creep on any of us. We must be vigilant, sober and fervent in spirit, in other to overcome. (Romans 12:11; 1 Peter 5:8).

**PRAYER**

1. Oh Lord, remove every seed of the sin of backsliding in me, in Jesus' name.
2. Oh Lord, grant me grace to follow you till the end and love you more and more.
3. I received new grace for the race ahead of me, in Jesus' name.
4. Father, give me fresh fire of the baptism of the Holy Spirit. I receive fresh power in Jesus' name.

## NOTES

# NOTES

## Study 15

# THE PILGRIM'S MENTALITY

**TEXT: 1 PETER 1:13-17; 2:11-12; HEBREWS 11:7-10**

Christians are strangers and pilgrims in this world. This means that we can be described as travelers, emissaries or ambassadors who are on a temporary assignment here on earth and can return to our homeland in heaven at any moment. This understanding is expected to regulate all of our affairs on earth. As Tertullian, one of the early Christians, once said, "And so it is that when a man walks along a road, the lighter he travels, the happier he is; equally, on his journey of life, a man is more blessed if he does not pant beneath a burden of riches." Thomas A. Kempis, another believer of note counseled, "Let temporal things serve your use, but the eternal be the subject of your desire.

This reminds me of an interesting encounter that John Wesley, founder of Methodism, had. A wealthy plantation owner once invited the revered minister to his home. The two rode their horses all day, seeing just a fraction of all the man owned. At the end of the day the plantation owner proudly asked, "Well, Mr.

Wesley, what do you think?" After a moment of silence, Wesley replied, "I think you are going to have a hard time leaving all this."

This is very instructive. While there is nothing wrong in being blessed on earth, believers must realize that we do not belong here. Therefore, we must conduct our activities and aspirations with the following components of the pilgrim's mentality:

### 1. Avoid attachment to worldly achievements - Colossians 3:1-2

Many of us live as if it is only in this world that our hope ends. We have too much attachment to things and we have forgotten that we are pilgrims, strangers and sojourners on earth.

### 2. Never feel at home in this world - Philippians 3:20

"Our citizenship is in heaven." If we are going to make it to heaven, we need to have this mentality that though we are living here on earth, we do not belong to this earth. We are running a race to our heavenly home. Our citizenship is of heaven because that is where we actually belong.

### 3. You are an alien/stranger here – Hebrews 11:13

Hebrews 11:13 reads: "These all died in faith, not having

received the promises, but having seen them afar off were assured of them, embraced them and confessed that they were strangers and pilgrims on the earth"

Part of our pilgrim's mentality is to recognize that we are "strangers" and we should live like it.

**Consider these characteristics of strangers:**

- Strangers have no permanent abode.
- Strangers have no permanent structures.
- Strangers live in borrowed houses, borrowed lands, and borrowed countries.
- Strangers are always mindful of their permanent home, where nothing is borrowed.
- Strangers are always thinking about the family members they left behind and are missing.
- Strangers prefer to gather things they can easily dispose of.
- Strangers have no serious attachment.

### 4. You are a seed of Abraham, with no abiding city on earth – Galatians 3:29

Hebrews 11:8-10 narrates, "By faith Abraham obeyed when he was called to go out to the place which he would receive as an inheritance. And he went out, not knowing where he was going. By faith he dwelt in the land of promise as in a foreign country, dwelling in tents with Isaac and Jacob, the heirs with him of the same promise; for he waited for the city which has foundations, whose builder and maker is God."

Abraham had the pilgrim's mentality and he was living in tents, not building permanent structures because he knew that he was a pilgrim. And as a true pilgrim with the right priorities, Abraham pitched his tent but built an altar to God.

Similarly, all heavenly pilgrims know that they have no abiding city here. They call no country their permanent home. They are aware that their real home is heaven above, beyond the skies, where angels and other saints are waiting to welcome on us into this joy of our spiritual inheritance in Christ.

### 5. You are a Levite unto God – Deuteronomy 18:1-2

The Levites had no earthly inheritance, because God himself was their inheritance. Christians have been told that we are a "chosen people" belonging to God (1 Peter 2:9). Our inheritance is God and the crowns that never fade away.

### 6. Money and possessions are tools for God's glory

"Command those who are rich in this present age not to be haughty, nor to trust in uncertain riches but in the living God, who gives us richly all things to enjoy. Let them do good, that they be rich in good works, ready to give, willing to share, storing up for themselves a good foundation for the time to come, that they may lay hold on eternal life" (1 Timothy 6:17-19).

The true pilgrim recognizes that the money and possessions in his hand are tools given to him or her by God to do the following:

1. To be rich in good works – assisting those who don't have, evangelism, church building/planting, building hospitals, schools, building and supporting orphanages etc.

2. Build a home in heaven and lay hold on eternal life by donating generously to God's work.

3. Shared for spreading of the gospel: supporting missions and missionaries, assisting media ministry and other ministries of the church.

Indeed, the more holdings we have on earth, the likely we lose our pilgrim's mentality and we forget that we are citizens of another world. Pilgrims are unattached to their money, possessions, positions and power. They realize that those things are transient. They are conscious that they are TRAVELLERS, NOT SETTLERS.

## PRAYERS

1. Lord, help me to live always with the consciousness that I am a stranger on earth.

2. Father, destroy every entanglements that seek to destroy my soul.

3. Lord, fill me with grace to make proper use of all the resources you bless me with on earth.

# NOTES

# NOTES

www.ingramcontent.com/pod-product-compliance
Lightning Source LLC
LaVergne TN
LVHW010105110826
845155LV00028B/490

*9781952098154*